Willis Boyd Allen

In the Morning

Willis Boyd Allen
In the Morning
ISBN/EAN: 9783744652001

Printed in Europe, USA, Canada, Australia, Japan

Cover: Foto ©Thomas Meinert / pixelio.de

More available books at **www.hansebooks.com**

IN THE MORNING.

BY

WILLIS BOYD ALLEN.

Den Abend lang währet das Weinen,
Aber des Morgens die Freude.
   LUTHER'S VERSION.

Hear what the Morning says, and believe that.
   EMERSON.

NEW YORK:
ANSON D. F. RANDOLPH AND CO.
38 WEST TWENTY-THIRD STREET.
1890.

Copyright, 1890,
BY WILLIS BOYD ALLEN.

University Press:
JOHN WILSON AND SON, CAMBRIDGE.

To my Mother.

CONTENTS.

	PAGE
AT CHRYSTEMESSE-TYDE	9
VITA NUOVA	11
NOT IN THE WHIRLWIND	15
DIAPASON	17
CHAMOUNIX	20
IN THE MORNING	22
MARIGOLD	25
"SEVENTEEN, EIGHTEEN, MAID'S A-WAITING!"	27
TO M——, ON HER BIRTHDAY	29
"YOURS TRULY"	30
A SERMON BY A LAY PREACHER	32
IN SOMNO VERITAS	36
THALATTA	38
UNKNOWN	39
MY CROSS	41
A VALENTINE	42
WHITE PINK	44
APRILLE	45
MAY	46

	PAGE
August	47
Carlo's Christmas	48
The Sun was Red and Low	50
Two Visions	52
My Creed	54
Again?	55
Pansy	56
Golden-Rod	57
To Margaret, on St. Valentine's Day	58
To a Very Small Pine	59
Mosses	61
The Mount of the Holy Cross	63
Christmas Snow	64
The "Creation"	65
The Happy Valley	67
Dollie's Spring	71
The Third Day	73
The Seventh Day	73
Fern Life	75
Its Home	75
At School	76
Asleep	76
A Cradle-Song of the Night Wind	77
The Chime	77
The Hymn of the Northern Pines	78
At Last	79

Contents.

	PAGE
PAUSES AND CLAUSES	80
TO M——, WITH A COPY OF "THE PETERKIN PAPERS"	81
MEMORIAL POEM	83
DANDELION	90
MARJORIE	92
PRIMROSE	94
CONTENT	96
WITH A SMALL LETTER-OPENER	98
SEA-GIRLS	102
HOMEWARD	104
A NONSENSE-SONG FOR M——	107
TRANSLATIONS	113
In the North-land	113
A Lovely Flower	113
Eagerly I cry	114
He who for the first Time	114
Little Maid	115
It was as if the Heavens	115
IN MORNING-LAND	117
SIC ITUR AD ASTRA	119
THE COMET, NOVEMBER, 1882	121
"HIS STAR"	122
"LICHT, MEHR LICHT!"	124
PSALM LXXX	126
UNTO THE PERFECT DAY	127

Contents.

	PAGE
HYMN FOR CHRISTMAS EVE	128
BLIND	130
REFUGE	133
GUIDO RENI'S "ECCE HOMO"	135
ON CHRISTMAS EVE	136
BY NIGHT	139
"STAR OF BETHLEHEM"	141
"BLESSED"	143
A CHRISTMAS PASTORAL	146
THE FOURTH WATCH	148
"WITH YOU ALWAY"	151
DECEMBER 31	152
IN MY ARM-CHAIR	154

AT' CHRYSTEMESSE-TYDE.

TWO sorrie Thynges there be, —
    Ay, three:
A Neste from which ye Fledglings have been
    taken,
    A Lamb forsaken,
A Petal from ye Wilde Rose rudely shaken.

Of gladde Thynges there be more, —
    Ay, four:
A Larke above ye olde Neste blithely singing,
    A Wilde Rose clinging
In safety to ye Rock, a Shepherde bringing
A Lamb, found, in his arms, — and
    Chrystemesse
    Bells a-ringing.

IN THE MORNING.

VITA NUOVA.

A DESERT, treeless, boundless,
   The low sun round and red,
Air stifling, moveless, soundless —
   And I alone with my dead.

Her head lay on my shoulder,
   The crimson light ebbed fast;
Her face grew paler, colder —
   The face of my own dead Past.

Then darkness, black and frightful,
   Dropped from the eastern sky,
With never a star, but a night-full
   Of horrors creeping by.

In the Morning.

I saw how fiercely glistened
    Their mad eyes, two by two, —
They screamed, and as I listened
    They laughed like a demon crew.

See how that huge hyena
    Grows bolder than the rest —
Slinks — snarls — in the arena,
    For the corpse upon my breast!

I laughed like the brutes around me,
    I snarled on my stony bed,
I severed the ties that bound me
    And gnashed upon the dead.

The tawny-sided creatures,
    Red claw and dripping fang,
The hideous, grinning features,
    The awful mirth that rang, —
All vanished. Starless, boundless,
    The night stretched o'er my head.
In the gray dawn, soulless, soundless,
    I sat alone with my dead.

Vita Nuova.

Then rustling forms drew nearer.
   By the faint approaching day
The frightful things grew clearer, —
   Great, unclean birds of prey
And carrion beasts, that waited
   Until, on the booty rare,
Their hunger foul should be sated
   With my poor Past, lying there.

Oh, I, too, sullen-hearted,
   No word of anguish said;
Till bird and beast departed
   I waited — dumb — by the dead.

The white east flickered with fire,
   A lark flew singing by,
The glad light mounted higher,
   Up-spread o'er all the sky.

My burden, fair and human,
   Still rested on my hands,
When lo! a gracious Woman,
   Swift walking o'er the sands,

Until she stood before me,
    Breathed words of hope and cheer;
Her radiant eyes were o'er me,
    Her presence warm and near,

And at her voice — oh, wonder! —
    The dead herself awoke;
The birds no longer shunned her,
    She smiled, and moved, and spoke,
Then, "FUTURE" named, to guide me
    She softly sprang away;
The Woman stayed beside me —
    Sun rose — it was full day.

NOT IN THE WHIRLWIND.

 POET sat in his oaken chair,
    The pen in his eager hand,
Awaiting the voice that should declare
    His Lord's divine command.

The sad winds sobbed against the pane,
    The tempest's tramp he heard
As it scourged the night with a hissing rain —
    But the Poet wrote never a word.

Then came a burst of martial mirth,
    And mighty cannon roared
Till they shook the beams of the steadfast earth —
    'T was not the voice of the Lord.

In the Poet's heart a memory rose
   Of love's first passionate thrill
That, kindling, grows as the red fire glows —
   But the pen was idle, still;

When lo, a timid voice at the door,
   And a child, with sweet delight,
Called "Father!" and "Father!" over and
     o'er —
   The poem was written that night.

DIAPASON.

ON the crags of a far-off mountain-
    top
  At earliest dawn a snowflake fell;
The North Wind stooped and cried to her,
    "Stop!
  There is room in my icy halls to dwell!"
The snowflake gleamed like a crystal clear,
Then wept herself to a single tear,
Paused, trembled, and slowly began to glide
Adown the slopes of the mountain-side.

Desolate ledges, frost-riven and bare,
  A tiny rivulet bore on their breast;
Cloud-gray mosses and lichens fair
  Mutely besought her to slumber and rest.
The rivulet shone in the morning sun,
And touching them tenderly, one by one,

In the Morning.

With dewy lips, like the mountain mist,
Each waiting face as she passed she kissed.

Among the shadows of pine and fir
   A stream danced merrily on her way;
A thrush from his hermitage sang to her:
   "Why dost thou haste? Sweet messenger, stay!"
The noontide shadows were cool and deep,
The pathway stony, the hillside steep,
The bird still chanted with all his art —
But the stream ran on, with his song in her heart.

Through broadening meadow and corn-land bright,
   Past smoke-palled city and flowery lea,
A river rolled on, in the fading light,
   Majestic, serene, as she neared the sea.
The sins and uncleanness of many she bore
To the outstretched arms of the waiting shore,
Till moonlight followed the sunset glow
And her crimson waves were as white as snow.

On the lonely ledges of Appledore
   I listen again to the ocean's song,
And lo! in its music I hear once more
   The North Wind's clarion, loud and long.
In that solemn refrain that never shall end
The murmurs of swaying fir-trees blend,
The brooklet's merry ripple and rush,
The evening hymn of the hermit thrush,
The undertone of the mountain pine, —
The deep sweet voice of a love divine.

CHAMOUNIX.

WITHIN Thy holy temple have I strayed
E'en as a weary child, who from the heat
And noonday glare hath timid refuge sought
In some cathedral's vast and shadowy aisle,
And trembling, awestruck, croucheth in his rags
Where high upreared a mighty pillar stands.

Mine eyes I lift unto the hills, from whence
Cometh my help. The murmuring firs stretch forth
Their myriad tiny crosses o'er my head;
Deep rolls the organ peal of thunder down
The echoing vale, while clouds of incense float
Around the great white altar set on high.

So lift my heart, O God, and purify
My thought, that when I walk once more
Amid the busy, anxious, struggling throng,
One cup of water from these springs of life,
One ray of sunlight from these golden days,
One jewel from the mountain's spotless
    brow,
As tokens of Thy beauty, I may bear
To little ones who toil, and long for rest.

IN THE MORNING.

'TWAS morn,
    And day was born.
    Bright in the west the stars
        still burned,
But ever, as the great earth turned,
The eastern mountain-tops grew dark
Against the rosy heaven — and hark !
A single note from flute-toned thrush
Drops downward through the twilight hush ;
Half praise, half prayer, I heard the song :
    "Oh, sweet, sweet,
Oh, life is sweet, and joy is long ! "

    The sun
    Touched one by one
The firs along the distant crest, —
A silent host, with lance at rest ;

In the Morning.

Flashed all the world with jewels rare,
Quivered with joy the maiden-hair
Beside the brook that downward sprang
And rippling o'er its mosses, sang
With silvery laugh the same glad song:
    "Oh, sweet, sweet,
Oh, life is sweet, and joy is long!"

    When lo!
    Swift, to and fro,
A sombre shadow crossed its path,
Deep thunders rolled in awful wrath,
The thrush beneath the fir-trees crept,
The maiden-hair bowed low and wept;
The heavens were black, the earth was gray,
The hills all blanched in the spectral day, —
The night-wind rose, and wailed this song:
    "Oh, long, long,
Oh, joy is fleeting, life so long!"

    Behold,
    A shaft of gold
Shot through the wrack of cloud and storm,
The heart of heaven beat quick and warm;

From bird and stream, with myriad tongue,
The glad day carolled, laughed, and sung.
'T was morning still! Her tear-drops bright
The maiden-hair raised to the light;
I heard, half prayer, half praise, the song:
　　　" Oh, sweet, sweet,
Oh, life is sweet, and joy is long!"

MARIGOLD.

MARIGOLD, marigold, wi' thy wee
    cup o' gold,
  What is it mak's thee sae bonnie
    an' gay?
Sunshine has drappit, an' filled up my cup o'
    gold
  Fu' to the brim wi' the licht o' the day.

Marigold, marigold, surely ye canna hold
  A' the sweet sunshine 'at draps frae the
    sky!
Nay, I 've a muckle o' licht 'at I winna hold,
  Saved up for you an' for ithers to try.

Marigold, marigold, stan'in' there a' sae bold,
  What's in thy een, 'at mak's 'em sae
    bright?
I keep 'em wide open, stan'in' here a' sae
    bold,
  Luikin' at heaven frae mornin' to nicht.

Marigold, marigold, bairnie wi' cup o' gold,
   What 's i' thy hert, 'at mak's thee sae strang?
Trust i' the One 'at gave me my cup o' gold
   Lattin' Him love me, a' the day lang.

"SEVENTEEN, EIGHTEEN, MAID'S A-WAITING!"

EIGHTEEN years ago the sunshine
Laughed to find a baby face;
Laughed to see the blue eyes sober,
In that golden, glad October,
Softly kissed the wisps of hair,
Softly kissed, and lingered there,
Like an answer to a prayer,
Like a whispered benediction,
Token bright of heavenly grace.

Standing on life's sunlit threshold,
Gazing forth with eyes of blue
On the great round world before her,
On the kind skies brooding o'er her, —
From the baby hair the light
Never has departed quite;

Still it lingers, pure and bright.
Yes, the little maid is waiting,
With a purpose grand and true;

Waiting for whate'er the Father
Calls His child to do and bear;
Waiting, as a thirsty flower
Waits the morning dew and shower.
Summers come and summers go,
Sparrows flutter to and fro,
Autumn breezes murmur low;
" Seventeen, eighteen, Maidie's waiting,
With the sunshine in her hair!"

TO M——, ON HER BIRTHDAY.

WITH A CHESS-BOARD.

OUR turn to move again, dear,
    I' the gude auld game ca'd Life ;
It's a warstle o' joy an' pain, dear,
A mixin' o' lauchter an' strife.

An' I fain wad be yer knight, dear,
    To serve ye the livelong day ;
Ready in armor to fight, dear,
    To live or to dee, as ye say.

Near at han' i' the gloamin' I 'd bide, dear,
    I' saddle at gray o' dawn —
Na, na, I 'm no worthy to ride, dear,
    Lat me be the White Queen's pawn !

"YOURS TRULY."

"Yours truly," she signs the note; ah, me!
   How little she dreams what that would be
To him who, trembling, reads the line, —
What if, indeed, she were truly mine!

What visions those two dear words can bring
To the lonely heart that is hungering
For a single touch of her dainty hand,
One swift, shy glance he could understand,

And know that the formal greeting sent
But half concealed what the writer meant, —
That she gave, throughout the eternities,
Her own sweet self, to be truly his!

There, there! — that fire, how it smokes —
   what, tears?
I'll answer her letter —

             "Dear Friend, I've fears
Your kind invitation I can't accept; still
I'll come if it's possible.
             Yours truly,   W<small>ILL</small>."

A SERMON BY A LAY PREACHER.

THE morning of Sabbath; a city at rest,
But waking serenely and donning its best,
For the warm March sun already is high.
Above, the arch of a white-blue sky;
Brown earth, with a touch of green, below;
Elm-boughs, uptost with a lift superb;
The melting ice and grimy snow
Playing meadow from curb to curb,
With small mud-rills in place of brooks,
And a sewer for sea!
                        Ah, hold, my friend,
I grant how childish-foolish it looks,
But perhaps they 've faith for the very end, —
For streams and sewers, greatest and least,
Find ocean at last, in the misty East.

A Sermon by a Lay Preacher.

The good people all are off to the churches,
While I, left here in the idlest of lurches,
Must seek a preacher to preach me a sermon,
Ordained with open-air dews of Hermon;
A discourse conservative, grave, edifying,
And — come, sir, no laughing! I really am trying
To find, if I can, the road steep and narrow;
Ah, here he comes, flying, a straw in his bill!
I'll beg him take pulpit; now hear, if you will,
    A sermon preached by a sparrow.

"My text" — hear the bird! — "I take
From the street," — that's better, — "and make
    Application as follows:
Down there where my comrades are basking,
There's food to be had for the asking, —
    Understand me, — no shirking,
    Our *asking* means *working*, —
    Each swallows
The meal that's laid on his plate,
Content with enough. There's my mate,

Her feathers a-fluff in the sun,
That brownest, prettiest one —
Your pardon! I ought to be preaching.
This, sir, is the gist of my teaching:
We sparrows take things as they come,
From four A. M. until six,
We work (using straw without bricks);
We stop now and then for a crumb
Thrown down by a child; full of cheer,
We twitter throughout the whole year,
Investing in no loans of trouble
Where the borrower always pays double."

But your text was the Street, my good bird.
This sounds like the Bible! —
      "I've heard
That life was the same, sir, in each;
And, though you want me to preach,
You'll find that men, fowls, and book,
     If you look,
Are all connected together, —
In short, are birds of a feather;
And from a genuine sermon
You'll learn, sir, — this I'm firm on, —

The same Hand guides and governs all
Which holds us sparrows when we fall."

No more.   Before I could even remind him
Of lack of an adequate exhortation,
Proper pauses, and peroration,
He was off, his straw streaming far behind him.

His advice — well, certainly not very new,
Yet perhaps worth trying, I think — don't you?

IN SOMNO VERITAS.

I DREAMED that I sat in my chamber
   And watched the dancing light
Of the blaze upon my hearthstone,
   And the red brands, glowing bright.

I listened to the rustle
   Of the flames that rose and fell,
And I dreamed I heard a whisper,
   A voice I knew full well.

The room no more was lonely,
   A Presence sweet was there,
A girlish figure, standing,
   Beside my own arm-chair.

In Somno Veritas.

I dreamed I spoke, and trembling
   Lest she should prove to be
The creature of a vision,
   I bade her sit by me.

Her grave brown eyes she lifted,
   Her dear hand placed in mine, —
The air was sweet with incense
   Of odorous birch and pine, —

And as we watched together
   Those eager, dancing flames,
We talked of days forgotten,
   And spoke our childish names.

I dreamed that heaven seemed nearer,
   The skies a lovelier blue,
Then — was it still a vision? —
   I dreamed my dream came true!

THALATTA.

FAR over the billows unresting forever
    She flits, my white bird of the sea,
Now skyward, now earthward, storm-drifted, but never
  A wing-beat nearer to me.

With eye soft as death or the mist-wreaths above her
  She timidly gazes below;
Oh, never had sea-bird a man for her lover,
  And little recks she of his woe.

One sweet, startled note of amazement she utters,
  One white plume floats downward to me;
Far over the billows a snowy wing flutters —
  Night — darkness — alone with the sea.

UNKNOWN.

HERE'S a star a-light in the gloam-
    ing,
  A gleam in the skies above;
There's a flower at rest on her bosom, —
  On the heart of her I love.

What says the star of the twilight?
  What is the song of the flower?
A cloud has covered the star-beam;
  The blossom lived but an hour.

Nay, 't is the infinite heaven,
  The depth beyond, that speak;
'T is the heart that throbs 'neath the blossom,
  Not the lip nor the fair white cheek.

The voice of the heavens is tender,
   Its whisper is fond and low;
But the voice of the heart that is throbbing —
   Its message I cannot know.

MY CROSS.

NLY a tiny cross;
    She plucked it from a mountain fir,
    And wreathing it in soft, gray moss,
Gave it in memory of her, —
        Yet — 't is a cross!

    Only a soft, gray cross;
But, half-concealed, full many a thorn
Lay waiting there, beneath the moss,
To pierce the bosom where 't is worn,
        This wee, sweet cross.

    Only a thorny cross,
Unconscious of the pain it gives;
Lifeless the fir, faded the moss,
Yet, while the hand that plucked them lives,
        It is my cross.

A VALENTINE.

F but the furry catkin small
    Could speak with gentle voice
    And bid the sad, Rejoice!
A pussy-willow should be all
    My valentine.

If but the golden daffodil,
    With many a cheerful word,
    Could tell what it hath heard
By meadow, wood, or murmuring rill,
    It should be mine.

If but the valley-lilies pure
    Could whisper in thine ear
    A message thou wouldst hear,
Of One whose promises are sure,
    Whose love divine,

A Valentine.

Such flowers my valentine should be.
   Yet sought I none of those, —
   Only one crimson rose
To bear its Maker's heart to thee, —
   Lo, it is thine !

WHITE PINK.

THE maiden left a timid kiss
    Upon the mossy stone;
  Her lover true, the maiden knew,
Would seek and find his own.

The lover never came again,
    Nor guessed the woe he wrought;
Day after day neglected lay
    The maiden's kiss, unsought.

At length, upspringing from the moss
    Through kindly sun and shower,
Its petals fair unfolded there
    This gentle, snow-white flower.

APRILLE.

APRILLE, alacke!
    With sunnie laugh her snow-white
        cloke flung backe,
    And gailie cast aside;
        Then cryed,
With little wilfulle gustes of raine,
Because she could not have her cloke againe.

MAY.

OVER the hilltop and down in the meadow-grass
   Heaven like dew on the waking earth lies:
Part of it, dear, is the blue of these violets;
   Best of it all I find in your eyes.

AUGUST.

AUGUST, the month of virgins, is at hand.
    Shrill-voiced, the locust pipes a-field;
With flash of burnished shield
Hovers the dragon-fly athwart the stream;
Like sea-bird slumbering in mid-day dream
Floats one white cloud above the drowsy land.
August, the month of virgins, is at hand.

Silent upon the shore sits Dorothy, —
    Scarce heeds the softly murmurous tide,
    Fair sky, nor aught beside;
Gazing afar, half troubled, half content,
Awaits with folded hands a message sent
Across the gleaming, restless, longing sea, —
Silent upon the shore sits Dorothy.

CARLO'S CHRISTMAS.

MAY I come to your side, dear Mistress?
   I am only a dog, you see,
And the Christmas joy and gladness
   Perhaps are not meant for me.

Yet I think the Master would let me,
   If I only begged to eat
The crumbs that fell from His table,
   And to lie at His blessèd feet.

I have heard the wonderful story
   Of the sleeping flocks by night,
Of Bethlehem and the angels
   And the one Star, shining bright;

And I've longed, when I heard the story,
   A shepherd-dog to be,
For then it might seem that Christmas
   Was partly meant for me.

But I only look up at the Master
   With a life that is veiled and dumb,
Content to share with the sparrow
   His love, and the falling crumb.

May I lie at your feet, dear Mistress?
   I am only a dog, you see,
But if I may serve you and love you,
   Why, that is Christmas for me!

THE SUN WAS RED AND LOW.

ON her palace porch a Princess —
   The sun was red and low —
At her feet a subject kneeling —
Sweet, far-off bells were pealing —
   He rose and turned to go.
"I give you my love!" quoth the Princess
   To the subject, bending low.

Ah, Goldenhair, what hast thou given! —
   The sun is round and red —
As thou standest there in the portal,
A Princess' love, to a mortal! —
   The bells toll for the dead —
A kiss from the lips of the Princess,
   But never a word she said.

Still radiant stood the Princess —
 The bells no longer tolled —
At her feet the subject kneeling —
The far-off chimes were pealing
 Their sweet notes as of old —
"I give you my love!" quoth the Princess;
 And the sun was a crown of gold.

TWO VISIONS.

 A VISION of Morn, — the dew's on
    the grass,
  The ocean's aflame, and a sweet
    fisher-lass
  On its bosom's unrest is afloat;
The sunlight is fair on her shy, upturned face,
As she dips the bright oars with the daintiest
    grace,
  And the prow of her snowy-white boat
Its way urges softly through each foaming
    crest,
Like sea-bird, wings fluttering, closing to rest;
In her eyes shines the light of the glad day,
    new-born, —
  The pure, gentle Spirit of Morn.

A Vision of Night, — the silvery stars
Alight in the East, ere its golden bars

Have imprisoned the slumberous sun ;
The sea hoarsely breathing, the wind all astir,
The sparrow crouched low in the boughs of the fir,
But she, the Beautiful One,
Is awake, oh, awake, with her glorious eyes
Star-lighted and deep as the shadowy skies,
O'er the mist of her draperies, fleecy and white,
The radiant Spirit of Night.

MY CREED.

HAT is my creed, you ask, dear?
    I look in your grave brown eyes
And believe — in your womanly sweetness,
  Your purity, clear as the skies.

I've faith — in your true, brave heart, dear,
  Your life, with its joys and tears;
And far beyond storm-mist and sunshine,
  Beyond weary days and long years,

I hope — in a Love that is waiting
  With infinite tenderness there
To comfort us both, you and me, dear,
  For the burden He gives us to bear.

AGAIN?

SIDE by side, from their misty home,
    Fell two bright drops of rain ;
  The storm-wind hurled them far
    apart,
  Never to meet again.

Hand in hand stood two dear friends,
  Hearts wrung with sudden pain ;
The storm-wind hurled them far apart, —
  Never to meet again?

PANSY.

LITTLE flower with golden heart,
Strange, sweet mystery thou art.
Who can tell the thoughts that lie
In the depths of thy dark eye!
Dost thou dream of other lands,
Waving palm-groves, burning sands,
Days of languor, twilights tender,
Glorious nights of Orient splendor?
Shy, sweet type of lovers' bliss,
Art thou an immortal kiss
By some fair sultana breathed,
To all faithful love bequeathed
By the tiny-sandalled bride,
Velvet-lipped, and starry-eyed?

GOLDEN-ROD.

O'ER the dusty roadside bending
  With its wondrous weight of gold,
Can it be the rod enchanted
  Midas used in days of old?

Hush! perchance it is a princess
  In the sunlight nodding there,
Spell-bound by the wicked fairy, —
  Sleepy little Golden-Hair!

Nay, it is Belshazzar's banquet,
  Where the drowsy monarch sups
With his swarm of courtiers, drinking
  From the sacred, golden cups.

See, I pluck his tiny kingdom —
  Long ago it was decreed —
And divide it, dear, between us,
  You the Persian, I the Mede.

TO MARGARET, ON ST. VALENTINE'S DAY.

WITH A ROSE.

MARGARET, pearl of dainty pearls,
   Fairest of dimpled daisies,
  My rose its velvet sail unfurls
 To bear thee love and praises.
It drifts from port, no longer mine —
Bring back, wee boat, my Valentine!

TO A VERY SMALL PINE.

WHAT song is in thy heart,
    Thou puny tree?
  Weak pinelet that thou art,—
Trembling at every shock,
Thy feebleness doth mock
    Thy high degree.

When rage o'er sea and land
    The tempests wild,
How canst thou e'er withstand
  Their might, or baffle them
  With that frail, quivering stem,
    Poor forest child?

Nay, wherefore scoff at thy
    Dimensions small?
For, folded close, I spy

A tiny bud, scarce seen
    Within its cradle green;
      And after all,

In ages yet to come
    Thy stately form,
No longer dwarfed and dumb,
    But chanting to the breeze
    Sublime, sweet melodies,
      Shall breast the storm!

Beneath thine outstretched arms
    Shall children rest;
While, safe from all alarms,
    Within thy shadows deep
    Wild birds their tryst shall keep
      And weave their nest.

May such a lot be his
    Who tends thee now!
With heavenly harmonies
    Serene amid his foes,
    Outstretching as he grows
      In root and bough.

MOSSES.

CHILDREN of lowly birth,
   Pitifully weak;
   Humblest creatures of the wood,
To your peaceful brotherhood
Sweet the promise that was given
Like the dew from heaven:
" Blessed are the meek,
They shall inherit the earth."

Thus are the words fulfilled:
Over all the earth
Mosses find a home secure.
On the desolate mountain crest,
Avalanche-ploughed and tempest-tilled,
The quiet mosses rest;
On shadowy banks of streamlets pure,
Kissed by the cataract's shifting spray,
For the bird's small foot a soft highway;

For the weary and sore distressed
In hopeless quest
Of a fabulous golden fleece,
Little sermons of peace.
Blessed children of lowly birth —
Thus they inherit the earth.

THE MOUNT OF THE HOLY CROSS.

DOWN the rocky slopes and passes
   Of the everlasting hills
   Murmur low the crystal waters
Of a thousand tiny rills;

Bearing from a lofty glacier
   To the valley, far below,
Health and strength for every creature,—
   'T is for them " He giveth snow."

On thy streamlet's brink the wild deer
   Prints with timid foot the moss;
To thy side the sparrow nestles,—
   Mountain of the Holy Cross!

Pure and white amid the heavens
   God hath set His glorious sign:
Symbol of a world's deliverance,
   Promise of a life divine.

CHRISTMAS SNOW.

HAT so merry as snow?
    Gleefully robing the grave old
       town
In garb fantastic of ermine and down;
Whispering at the window pane,
Then spreading its wee, white wings again
Till, alighting at last with noiseless feet,
On tiptoe in the muffled street
    It dances to and fro.

    What so pure as snow?
Flakes like the thoughts of a little child,
Undefiling and undefiled;
Wonderful, starry mysteries
Falling softly out of the skies,
Decking with white the bare, brown earth
In memory of the holy birth
    At Bethlehem, long ago.

THE "CREATION."

WINTER is past. The changing, softened sky,
The robin's cheery note, the sea-bird's cry,
The willow pussies peeping from their nest;
The modest sparrow, with his dappled breast,
Flitting beneath the lilacs by the wall;
The budding tree, the tender grass, with all
Its tiny hands uplifted to the sun,
Who reaches down and clasps them, one by one;
The mayflower sleeping on her snowy bed,
And while the night winds murmur, "She is dead!"
Her shy sweet eyes unclosing joyfully
As if she heard the "Talitha, cumi!"
The stream, escaping from the winter's wrath,
And leaping swiftly down its rocky path,

Or pausing in some shadowy, foam-flecked
 pool,
Among the nodding ferns and mosses cool;
The floating clouds, the fragrant earth, the
 sea,
With its low whispers of eternity, —
All join in one grand harmony of praise
To Him, Creator, Lord, Ancient of Days.

THE HAPPY VALLEY.

FAR away there sleeps a valley,
    Cradled by the mighty hills,
    Lulled to rest by sweetest music, —
Whispering winds and laughing rills.

Naught it knows of stormy passion,
    Pestilence, or war's alarms ;
O'er it graze the peaceful cloud-flocks,
    And the everlasting arms

Of the mountains, underneath it,
    Fold it closely to their breast,
While at nightfall, on its bosom,
    Golden moonbeams softly rest.

Seasons come and seasons go, —
Summer heats and winter's snow,
Spring's surprises, autumn's peace,
Indian-summer's golden fleece,

In the Morning.

Purple-bordered, crimson-clasped,
By a hand already grasped
That hath costlier treasures brought
Than the wandering Argonaut.

A solemn hush is in the air.
   Happy voices die away;
   Dark-robed fir-trees murmur, Pray! —
Pray for Summer, young and fair.
      Crosses wave,
      Souls to save,
      Chant a requiem o'er her grave.

Dead! the weeping autumn wind
   Shrouded her in fallen leaves;
   Dead! amid her golden sheaves, —
Pray — ye that are left behind!
      Crosses wave,
      Souls to save,
      Chant a requiem o'er her grave.

Pray ye, pray! for Summer lies
   Dead, upon the icy ground;
   Heap for her a snow-white mound,
While the winter wind replies:

Crosses wave,
Souls to save,
Chant a requiem o'er her grave.

Sweetly, through the low, sad murmur
   Of the fir-trees' requiem,
Flows a song of hope and gladness,
   Strong, triumphant over them.

Summer is not dead, but sleepeth!
   Soon the maiden shall arise,
And the world again be gladdened
   With the sunshine of her eyes.

Then the valley, too, shall waken
   From the pale trance of her night;
Breezes soft shall kiss her forehead,
   Radiant in the morning light.

Years may come and go, but ever
   Shall the valley rest among
Mountain mists and golden moonbeams;
   While the hills, with myriad tongue,

Lullabys shall croon above it,
    Streamlets laugh, and harebells chime,
Fir-trees murmur, cloud-lambs wander,
    Storms chant harmonies sublime.

And for those who love the valley
    Peace and rest are waiting there,
With the seasons onward moving,
    Each more gladsome, each more fair.

DOLLIE'S SPRING.

DEEP within a mountain forest
    Breezes soft are whispering
Through the dark-robed firs and
    hemlocks,
Over Dollie's Spring.

Swiftly glides the tiny streamlet,
    While its laughing waters sing
Sweetest song in all the woodland,
    " I — am — Dollie's — Spring ! "

In the dim wood's noontide shadow
    Nod the ferns, and glistening
With a thousand diamond dew-drops,
    Bend o'er Dollie's Spring.

Shyly on its mossy border
    Blue-eyed Dollie, lingering,
Views the sweet face in the crystal
    Depths of Dollie's Spring.

Years shall come and go, and surely
  To the little maiden bring
Trials sore and joys uncounted,
  While, by Dollie's Spring,

Still the firs shall lift their crosses
  Heavenward, softly murmuring
Prayers for her, where'er she wander, —
  Far from Dollie's Spring.

THE THIRD DAY.

LINES SENT WITH A FOSSIL FROND.

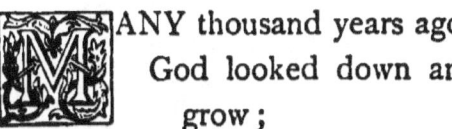ANY thousand years ago
   God looked down and bade me
     grow;
Why it was, I never knew —
Now I see it was for you!

THE SEVENTH DAY.

SENT WITH A CLUSTER OF MAIDEN-HAIR FERNS.

DOUBTLESS you are much surprised
That we are not fossilized,
Geologic, or antique, —
Only little ferns and meek.
Yet we grew at His command,
Touched by that same loving Hand

In the Morning.

Which the day from night divided,
Planets on their courses guided,
Set on high the firmament,
Alps from Alps asunder rent,
All the earth with life invested;
And He made us while He — "*rested.*"

FERN LIFE.

I. Its Home.

WITHIN a shadowy ravine
    Far hidden from the sun,
A fern its wee, soft fronds of green
    Unfolded, one by one.

From morn till eve no twittering flock
    Nor insect hovered nigh:
Its cradle was the lichened rock,
    The storm its lullaby.

By night above the dark abyss
    The stars their vigils kept,
And white-winged mists stooped low to kiss
    The baby, while it slept.

II. At School.

Weeks passed away; the tiny fern
    Frond after frond unfurled,
And waited patiently to learn
    Its mission in the world.

By fir-trees draped in mosses gray
    The willing fern was taught,
And once each day a single ray
    Its sunny greeting brought.

III. Asleep.

Her cradle songs the North Wind sung
    And whispered far and wide,
Until a thousand harebells swung
    Along the mountain side.

She sung of far-off twilight land,
    Moss-muffled forests dim,
And, to her mountain organ grand,
    The aged pine-trees' hymn.

IV. A Cradle-Song of the Night Wind.

The pines have gathered upon the hill
   To watch for the old-new moon;
I hear their murmuring — "Hush, be still!
   'T is coming — coming soon!"

The brown thrush sings to his meek brown
    wife
   Who broods below on her nest:
"Of all the world and of all my life
   'T is you I love the best!"

But the baby moon is wide awake,
   And its eyes are shining bright;
The pines in their arms this moon must take
   And rock him to sleep to-night.

V. The Chime.

Softly swinging to and fro,
   Harebells tinkle, sweet and low!.
     All the world is fast asleep,
     Birds and folks and woolly sheep;

Far above us towers the mountain;
Far below, an unseen fountain
   From its rocky cradle deep,
   Like a child, laughs in its sleep.
All our faces shyly hidden,
As the fir-trees oft have bidden,
   Softly bending, sweet notes blending,
      Moonbeams climbing,
      Wee bells chiming,
Harebells tinkle, star-gleams twinkle,
      To and fro,
      To and fro,
   Sweet — sweet and low.

VI. The Hymn of the Northern Pines.

   Sure — sure — sure —
Are the promises He hath spoken,
His word hath never been broken.
   Pure — pure — pure —
Are the thoughts and the hearts of His chosen,
As crystals the North Wind hath frozen.
   Strong — strong — strong —
Underneath are the arms everlasting;
On them our cares we are casting.

Long — long — long —
Have we sung of the life He doth give us —
His mercy and love shall outlive us.

VII. AT LAST.

FAR from its mountain home the fern
    Has found a resting-place ;
A maiden has begun to learn
    To love its winsome face.

But when at night the north winds smite
    Against the frosty pane,
The fern is listening with delight
    To hear their voice again.

For in their solemn murmuring
    The pine-trees chant once more,
The harebells chime, the thrushes sing,
    The mountain torrents roar ;

Again the dark-robed fir-trees stand
    About its mossy bed,
And hold aloft with trembling hand
    Their crosses o'er its head.

PAUSES AND CLAUSES.

TO MY LITTLE NIECE, KITTIE.

[With a Maltese Kitten.]

KITTIE MABEL, will you take
This gift, for the giver's sake?
Verse and song and roundelay
Will be yours this merry day;
Mine are all unfit to send,
Tattered rhymes, too poor to mend.

But, although I have n't any
Songs, my thoughts are swift and many.
All are flying straight to you,
And your heart, so sweet and true,
I am sure, dear, won't decline
This small, furry Valentine.

TO M——, WITH A COPY OF "THE PETERKIN PAPERS."

A BOSTON girl prefers a set of volumes that are uniform,
In Syriac, Chaldaic, Sanskrit, Arabic, or Cuneiform,
For these will test her paleontological ability,
And not insult her culture by superfluous facility.
She loves a scientific pedant, or, to use a synonyme,
A specimen, with printed name and label fair to pin on him.
Alas! I fear she will despise a book without a mystery,
That never once alludes to Art, or Mediæval History;

But as she is compelled each day to recognize and meet her kin,
I trust she will accept at least this tale of Mrs. Peterkin.

MEMORIAL POEM.

READ AT THE ANNUAL DINNER OF THE BOSTON LATIN SCHOOL ASSOCIATION, APRIL 29, 1886.

A LATIN-SCHOOL poem? 'T were easy to write
On a theme so suggestive an epic at sight,
An ode, full of fire, or, if that would n't do,
An Eclogue, or even a Georgic or two,
With allusions to classical roots, and Greek ponies
Hard ridden and worn — I confess that my own is.
A poet could scarce fail of making a hit,
Inspired by the presence of beauty and wit!

Alas, for the days of our ancestors bold,
When the wassail was drunk, brave stories were told,

While the mirth of the feasters grew louder and higher,
And the bard struck the quivering chords of the lyre,
Without an apology, blush, or evasion,
Or stammering reference to — "this occasion,"
As raising his voice o'er the tumult and din,
He recounted in song all the fights they'd been in.

Let bygones be bygones, the past be the past;
We live in the world of to-day, and at last
Society calls for less noise, more decorum,
Remarks less akin to the street than the forum;
Nay, mounting in civilization still higher,
The bard soon must go — perhaps even the lyre!
And if things should be ever at sixes and sevens,
There lies an appeal to his Honor Judge Devens.[1]

[1] Presiding at the Dinner.

And what, do you ask, is this tirade about?
Why not, as in Hunting the Snark, "leave
 that out"?
Ah, can I forget why we schoolmates are here?
How often we laugh when we'd fain hide a
 tear!
The ripples are bright on the waves of mid-
 ocean;
Eyes dance and smiles play over depths of
 emotion;
Oh, dear Alma Mater, be patient to-night,
Our hearts, misconstrued, thou canst trans-
 late aright!

How memory pictures bright scenes to us
 all! —
The old, shaky building, the school-room, the
 hall,
The way the grim doctor read Greek verbs
 and Latin,
The desk where he wrote and the chair that
 he sat in,
His upraised forefingers and forehead por-
 tentous,

The terror we felt when we found that he
    meant us;
Eyes gleaming below that great frontlet of
    hair, —
Ah, could we have known of what really was
    there,
And fathomed that grand heart, so gentle
    and true,
Beneath the stern front that bent o'er me
    and you!

Those lessons — how useless and tiresome
    they seemed,
While we "mulled" over Cæsar, drew pictures, and dreamed;
How Xenophon's mighty Anabasis came
To cloud our young lives, till we hated his
    name,
The characters playing strange pranks on the
    pages,
While still we droned on, "He — advanced
    — thirteen — stages."
We wished the Ten Thousand had all broken
    loose

Before they began on their endless σταθ-μούς;
We preferred that they would n't get on quite so fast;
We wished that their leader had not ἀνα-βάσ-ed;
But Xenophon brought them all safe to the sea,
He got out of the woods, and, at last, so did we.

Did you march on the Common? How proud were we then
To be reckoned in newspapers " two hundred men " !
How the uniforms shone as we wheeled o'er the grass —
No koh-i-noor gleams like those buttons of brass !
Our scabbards and sashes were artfully dangled,
And if they at times in our ankles got tangled,
The terror to others was full compensation
For dangers attending our perambulation.

Was it fun? There are those within reach
of my words
Who remember when ploughshares were
cleft into swords;
When hushed was the voice of youth's laugh-
ter and mirth,
As the flag, broken-winged, fluttered, bleed-
ing, to earth.
Are there men who will cherish their coun-
try's last breath?
Are there three hundred thousand who love
— to the death?
Hark! — the answering cry to that agonized
call —
And the Latin-School boys are the foremost
of all!

We have proved we've a banner, a country,
a God,
By thousands of arguments — under the sod!
Who knows if the dear boys who fell in the
fight
May not hold their reunion, as we do, to-
night?

From the morning-land fair, and a rest never
 ending,
Their voices, well-loved, with our own still
 are blending;
Hark! — can we not hear the sweet echoes
 to-day,
As from camp grounds afar comes the soft
 reveillé?

Oh, soldiers, still serving in ranks like their
 own,
But a little more quiet, more dignified, grown,
Still fighting from morning till set of the sun,
Each day new defeats or fresh victories won,
Pressing onward, undaunted still, shoulder to
 shoulder,
With our hearts growing young as our mus-
 kets grow older,
Let us take for our motto, emblazoned in
 light,
That stern old command of *Forward — Guide
 Right!*

DANDELION.

 A DANDELION in a meadow grew
    Among the waving grass and
      cowslips yellow;
Dining on sunshine, breakfasting on dew,
    He was a right contented little fellow.

Each morn his golden head he lifted straight,
    To catch the first sweet breath of coming
      day;
Each evening closed his sleepy eyes, to wait
    Until the long, cool night had passed away.

One afternoon, in sad, unquiet mood,
    I paused beside this tiny, bright-faced
      flower,
And begged that he would tell me, if he could,
    The secret of his joy through sun and
      shower.

He looked at me with open eyes, and said :
   "I know the sun is somewhere shining clear,
And when I cannot see him overhead,
   I try to be a little sun, right here !"

MARJORIE.

"OH, dear," said Farmer Brown, one day,
  "I never saw such weather!
The rain will spoil my meadow hay
  And all my crops together."
    His little daughter climbed his knee;
    "I guess the sun will shine," said she.

"But if the sun," said Farmer Brown,
  "Should bring a dry September,
With vines and stalks all wilted down,
  And fields scorched to an ember—"
    "Why, then, 't will rain," said Marjorie,
    The little girl upon his knee.

"Ah, me!" sighed Farmer Brown, that fall,
  "Now, what 's the use of living?

No plan of mine succeeds at all — "
"Why, next month comes Thanksgiving!
And then, of course," said Marjorie,
"We're all as happy as can be."

"Well, what should I be thankful for?"
Asked Farmer Brown. "My trouble
This summer has grown more and more,
My losses have been double,
I've nothing left — " "Why, you've got
me!"
Said Marjorie, upon his knee.

PRIMROSE.

N the meadow, cool and sweet,
 Where the cowslips bathe their
   feet,
On the banks of Scottish burns,
Down among the nodding ferns,
Where the shadows come and go,
Cheerful Primrose loves to grow.

Little flower she is, and meek;
And if she could only speak,
I am sure her words would be
Whispered very timidly.
Skylark, hush your joyous singing,
Bonnie harebells, cease your ringing,
Listen, listen, drowsy bee, —
Is the Primrose calling thee?

Primrose.

Tiny rootlets white and brown,
Leaves as soft as cygnet's down,
Fringèd petals, dainty pink,
Peeping o'er the burnie's brink, —
That is Primrose, sweet and true,
And I love her — do not you?

CONTENT.

"LITTLE Herb Robert, what makes
    you so pink?
  The daisy is taller and whiter."
"The sun came along, and, what do you
    think?
  It kissed me, and so I grew brighter."

"Grasshopper, why are you merry to-day?"
  "I always am glad, if you please, sir,
Because I can hop on the clover and hay,
  Nor have to fly up in the trees, sir."

"Sea-weed, poor creature! you're left high
    and dry,
  The tide has gone out; you are dying!"
"Ah, no, I am sure 't will come back by and
    by.
  I shall live, never fear; I'll keep trying."

Content.

"Song-sparrow, how can you sing all the day?"
"Sweet food to my young I am bringing,
And when I am working for them, in this way,
Of course I can never help singing."

"Child, leave the hot, dusty roadside, and come."
"I'd go, for I know that you love me;
But, please, I'd rather stay here, near my home,
For Papa's in there, just above me."

WITH A SMALL LETTER-OPENER.

TO W. B. W.

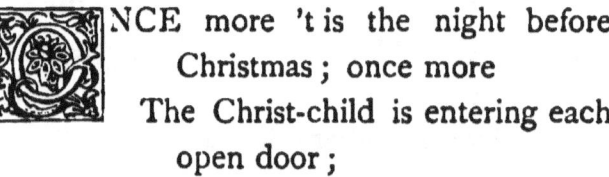NCE more 't is the night before
    Christmas; once more
The Christ-child is entering each
    open door;
The holly-bough glistens, the earth is all
    white,
In the jubilant heavens the Star is a-light.
May I sit by your hearthstone once more, as
    of old?
My story — a brief one — shall quickly be
    told.

We bring you no Sèvres nor Japanese Kaga,
But only an innocent kind of a dagger.
(Allow me a few editorial " we's,"
The plural is handy in rhymes such as these.)

With a Small Letter-opener.

The blade is no marvel, 't is not Muramasa —
("What's that?" No one knows. Ask
    your daughter, from Vassar.)
Nay, we must admit, if perchance you
    should ask us,
'T was forged in the States, and not at
    Damascus.
Too slim for a trinket, too large for a charm,
Too small for a weapon, too dull to do harm;
Too blunt for a bodkin, of life to deplete us,
'T would not even serve for Hamlet's
    quietus.
Cur igitur tibi gladiolum dabo —
Quemadmodum hoc explicare parabo?
Sie können nicht ganz die Verwerrung
    verstehen,
Ich will zum Puncte deswegen nun gehen.
Ce poignard petit est une clef de mon cœur,
Que je donne quelquefois à mon ami, ma
    sœur,
A celui, enfin, qui reçoit, dans mes lettres,
Les mots le plus tendres que je puis y mettre.
κἀγὼ πρὸς ὑμᾶς τὴν κλεῖδα λαβεῖν
ἐθέλειν ἐλπίζω καί με νῦν φιλεῖν.

(If once on a jingle like this voi entrate,
You must finish, or — ogni speranza lasciate!)
I wish I knew Indian, but somehow nobody
Seems ever to learn more than " Passamaquoddy,"
Or " Mooselucmaguntic," " Welokennebacook,"
" Oquossuc," " Musketequid," and " Quantibacook."
To compose in that language you will not deny
Is difficult. If you don't think so — just try.

'T is nonsense, dear friend, but I feel sure that you
Good-naturedly smile, and yet see 't is true.
Unconscious as Lady Macbeth in her walking,
We give in our letters more *self* than in talking.
Perhaps when our Father looks lovingly down

On our wandering footsteps in country and town,
Our burdens, our hindrances all, He can see,
And read in His wisdom more surely than we.
Far more than when kneeling by altar or crypt,
Our deeds make the record, in broad, cursive script.
Thank God that the Reader and Father are one,
That the poor, blotted copy-book, hardly begun,
Is read by Him only who wrote on the sand,
And the torn covers folded at last by His hand.
Hark! Christmas bells ring for the birth of the Son —
Good-night! May He help us and bless us each one.

SEA-GIRLS.

A FLUTTER of white
On Appledore's shoulder, —
The prettiest sight!
A flutter of white,
One by one they alight
On the dark, jutting bowlder;
A flutter of white
On Appledore's shoulder.

Six girls in a flock
Where the white sea is breaking
Against the gray rock.
Six girls in a flock —
Their gay voices mock
The din it is making;
Six girls in a flock
Where the white sea is breaking.

Sea-girls.

Each flutters and clings
To the torn granite edges, —
The merriest things!
Each flutters and clings.
Have they feathers and wings,
As they perch on the ledges?
Each flutters and clings
To the torn granite edges.

HOMEWARD.

A TWILIGHT SONG OF THE WHEEL.

AWAY from the office and desk at last,
  The business-haunted room,
The roar of a city, hurrying past,
  The heat, the worry, the gloom,
To the glorious red of the sunset sky,
  The sweet, cold wine of the air,
On the frozen road, my wheel and I,
  A dusty, rusty pair!

  Push — Push —
Two birds in a bush
Are laughing to see me hop;
  On, with a bound
  From the frozen ground,
With never a sway nor stop.

Over and over the pedals fly —
" Come on ! " to the twittering bird I cry,
　　As over and over the wheels fly past
　　　her ;
　　Over and over, still faster and faster,
On through the ice-cold stream of air,
On where the road is frozen and bare.

　　　Roll — Roll — Roll — Roll —
Silent and swift as a death-freed soul.
　　　　Glide — Glide —
　　　　　On the smooth, black tide
Of the ocean of night flowing in from the
　　　West,
Over and over, and on without rest,
Swifter and swifter, till over the crest
Of the hill, and down to the valley below,
Through the murk of the mist and the white
　　　of the snow —
Now my steed falters, as, breathless and
　　　slow,
Up the steep hillside he labors and grinds,
　　　Grinds — Grinds — Grinds — Grinds —
Across and across he turns and winds,

Sand-clogged and rock-hindered, without
    hope or faith,
No longer a soul, but a sin-burdened wraith —
Till, reaching the summit, he spurns the dark
    hill,
And onward he plunges, for good or for ill,
    Over and onward, and onward and over,
He reels and he spins like a jolly old rover.

    Roll — Roll — Roll — Roll —
Backward he flies to our one dear goal,
Where the whirling shall cease, and the rider
    shall rest,
  And soft, trembling lips to my own shall
    be pressed.
    Slow — Slow — Slow,
  Slowly — more slowly — we go —
What, darling, so far on the road to-night,
To welcome us both with your eyes' sweet
    light !
The wheel no longer has need to roam —
  Be quiet, old fellow ! we 're safe, safe at
    home.

A NONSENSE-SONG FOR M——.

FROM THE BACK OF THE NORTH WIND.[1]

I.

BREATHING, blowing,
    The cool breeze is blowing,
    High in the tree-tops,
  Low in the grasses,
  Softly it passes ;
  The daisies it kisses
  And never one misses,
And laughs at the buttercups,
    Breathing and blowing,
    Its blessing bestowing
    On all that it passes
    Among the low grasses
And daisies and buttercups,

---

[1] Suggested by George MacDonald's little book of that name.

Never one misses,
But each one it kisses.
Softer and fainter it grows,
Faintly and softly it blows,
  Breathing, sighing,
    Dying,
Sweetly and softly it goes,
  Goes — goes !

II.

Hark to the wind from the mountain-tops
    blowing !
  Raining, snowing,
Scattering ice-drops and crimson leaves
    blowing !
  Teasing the burnies
  With all their soft fernies,
  Bending and waving
  Among the green mosses ;
  Roaring and raving,
  The long hair it tosses
  Of each little maiden
  Beside the brown burnies

With crimson leaves laden
All bound for the sea,
With wee boaties laden,
All crimson to see,
And high in the tree-tops
It rushes and roars ;
It leaps from the hill-tops
And hurls with its might on the long, rocky
    shores
  The floods of the sea,
All the time roaring and shouting and
    blowing,
  Icy drops throwing,
    Blowing, snowing,
      It roars !

III.

What shall the Soft Breeze do for thee?
What shall I do with my faint, sweet blow-
    ing,
  Breathing, blowing,
  My blessing bestowing?

In the Morning.

> I pray thee, Soft Breeze,
> Do thou blow, for me!
> Stir in the trees
> And breathe in the grasses,
> The soft, low grasses,
> And when the tall buttercup,
> Tall in the grasses,
> Thy light foot passes,
> Gather for me
> A wee grain of gold from its treasures rare,
> A ray of the sunlight it treasures there;
> Then beg of the daisies a bit of their white,
> Pure, pure white,
> And two tiny petals, crimson tipped,
> Because in God's love they have just been dipped,
> And bearing the sunlight, the whiteness and love,
> Breathing, blowing,
> Fair blessings bestowing,
> Among the soft grasses
> And tree-tops above,
> High in the cloud-land's silvery sheen,
> Low in the winding valleys between,

Seek my wee girlie
Who's just thirteen,
With hair so curly,—
The curliest hair you ever have seen,
The brownest hair you ever have seen,—
With eyes so blue,
Like skies so blue,
And hide thy gifts in her heart so true,
For to-day she's just thirteen,
Thirteen.

IV.

What shall the Fierce Wind do for thee?
What shall I do, with my terrible roaring,
Raving, roaring,
Icy drops pouring?

I pray thee, Fierce Wind,
Do thou roar, for me!
Shatter the crags of the desolate mountain,
Scatter the drops of the trembling fountain,
Ride on the waves of the tossing sea,
Tossing and spouting,
Roaring and shouting;

In the Morning.

Snatch a bright leaf from the burnie's brink,
And a drop from the pool where the white lambs drink,
  A wisp of hair from the maiden fern,
  Bending over the laughing burn;
    The health of the seas,
    The life of the trees,
    The beauty of fernies,
    The faith of bright burnies,
Life and beauty and health and faith,
Whiteness and sunshine, love stronger than death,
  These to the maidie that 's just thirteen
  Shall all be given to-day, I ween, —
    Shall all be given,
    In blessing from Heaven, —
  For now she 's just thirteen,
    And her eyes are so blue,
    Sweet skies so blue,
    And her heart so true,
  And to-day she 's just thirteen,
    Thirteen.

TRANSLATIONS.

SONGS FROM HEINE.

IN the north-land standeth a pine-tree
  Alone, on a hill-top bare.
It sleepeth beneath a mantle
  Of snow and frost-work rare.

It dreameth long of a palm-tree
  Which, silent as a star,
On the burning desert mourneth
  In Orient lands afar.

A LOVELY flower thou seemest,
  So tender, sweet, and true;
And, as I gaze, steals o'er me
  A sadness strange and new.

Upon thy peaceful forehead
    I'd lay my hands, in prayer
That God may ever keep thee
    As tender, true, and fair.

EAGERLY I cry, awaking,
    "Cometh she to-day?"
Eventide — my sad heart, breaking,
    Speaks the answer, Nay!

In the night I know but sorrow
    Till the dawn's faint beam;
Mist-enwrapped, in each to-morrow,
    Agony of dream.

HE who for the first time loveth,
    Godlike, worlds of bliss doth rule;
He who twice that joy essayeth,
    Luckless wight — he is a fool.

Loving where no love returneth,
    Such a fool, alas! — am I;
Sun and moon and stars are laughing,
    I laugh, too, — *and die.*

Little maid, with lips so rosy,
   With thy blue eyes, sweet and clear,
All my thoughts to thee are flying,
   All my life is with thee, dear!

Slowly pace the leaden-footed
   Hours that mark the winter's night;
Ah, that I were now beside thee,
   Gazing, murmuring my delight!

Kisses would I press, my darling,
   On thy little hand to-night;
Nay — a tear should fall, unbidden,
   On thy little hand so white.

(Eichendorff.)

It was as if the heavens
   Had kissed the earth to rest,
And she lay dreaming of them
   With flowers upon her breast.

The fields and murmuring woodland
  Were bathed in fairest light,
So soft the breeze's whisper,
  So starry-clear the night!

On outspread wings uplifted
  My spirit fain would roam
Through cloudland realms unbounded,
  To rest at last — at home.

IN MORNING-LAND.

N Morning-land the radiant, rosy skies
    Each moment gleam with some
    new-born surprise,
Or flush with dawning hope ; the balmy air
Is laden with a thousand perfumes rare
And thrilled with chords of strange, sweet
    melodies.

On that blest shore, which all around us lies,
Peace reigns supreme, and joyous carols rise
From every shaded copse and pleasaunce fair
        In Morning-land.

Knowst thou the land? Wherever friendly
    eyes
Beam faith and constancy ; where true love
    flies,

Glad tidings of good-will and peace to bear;
Where service is divine, God everywhere, —
There dawns the perfect day that never dies
    In Morning-land.

SIC ITUR AD ASTRA.

 STOOD in a valley ; above me
    Uprose a mighty hill ;
The air was vibrant with music
    Of insect, bird, and rill.

The flowers among the grasses
    About my weary feet
Swung all their tiny censers,
    Till perfume, heavy-sweet,

Was shed abroad in the sunlight
    And wafted to and fro,
While droning bees at the altar
    Their *Aves* chanted low.

A soft breeze touched my forehead,
    And whispered, " Peace, be still ! "
But ever above me towered
    That silent, awful hill,

Whose peaks in mists were hidden,
   Whose slopes were brown and bare;
And yet, as I gazed, I murmured,
   "O God! If I were there!"

For I knew that the peace of the valley
   Was never meant for me;
And I longed for the mountain summit, —
   Its pure winds blowing free,

Its life of strength and vigor,
   Its thoughts of the good and true,
Its steadfast crags of granite
   In the far-off, heavenly blue.

I stand in the valley, and ever
   I gaze at the mountain bare,
And I long for a hand to help me —
   O God! That I were there!

THE COMET; NOVEMBER, 1882.

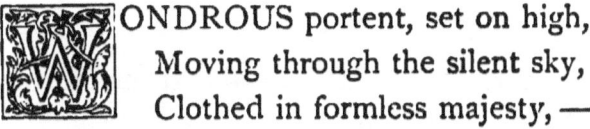ONDROUS portent, set on high,
Moving through the silent sky,
Clothed in formless majesty, —

Who can read those words of light
On the star-lit wall of night?
"*Mene, Tekel,*" dost thou write?

Nay, thou bright Star in the East,
O'er no haughty monarch's feast,
Prophet nor Chaldæan priest,

Doth thy gentle radiance shine;
Nobler resting-place is thine,
'T is a Baby's brow divine.

With the waning of the year
From afar thou dost appear,
Telling us that Christ is near.

"HIS STAR."

CHRISTMAS Eve — and the mellow light
    Of the Star in the East was aglow
O'er the Magi, hastening through the night,
    In the desert, long ago.

Christmas Eve — and the gentle light
    Of the Star in the East was aglow
O'er the lambs, asleep with their shepherds by night,
    On the hillside, long ago.

Christmas Eve — and the golden light
    Of the Star in the East was aglow
O'er a Baby's brow, in the holy night,
    In a manger, long ago.

Christmas Eve — and the blessed light
  Of the Star in the East is aglow,
As it shone of old, through the sweet, still
    night,
  O'er Bethlehem, long ago.

"LICHT, MEHR LICHT!"

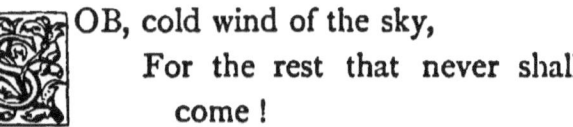OB, cold wind of the sky,
    For the rest that never shall come!
The stars have gathered on high,
    The moon's white lips are dumb,
And over her face like a shroud
Lies the wrack of the drifting cloud.

Moan, dark sea of the night!
    Fling up thine arms and implore
The heavens for light, sweet light, —
    One sparkle along the shore
From the sun that left thee to moan
In the horror of darkness — alone.

Shudder, thou one human soul,
    Forever alone in the night;

Whose billows unceasingly roll
   In desolate seeking for light !
The moon's white face is thine own,
Thine, thine the wind's monotone.
      Thyself art the night —
    O God, light, light !

PSALM LXXX.

"TURN us again, O God of Hosts, and cause
Thy face to shine."
When fades the light of day,
And night in silence steals across the sky,
We know it is not that the glorious sun
Has left his steadfast throne amid the heavens,
But that our little earth has turned away
And hid its face till morning shall appear.
So may we, in our blackest night of doubt
And troubled thought, return once more to
Thee,
Till Thou hast risen, O Sun of Righteousness,
And all the evil things of darkness born
Have fled before the shining of Thy face.

UNTO THE PERFECT DAY.

A MORNING-GLORY bud, entangled fast
   Amid the meshes of its winding stem,
Strove vainly with the coils about it cast,
   Until the gardener came and loosened them.

A suffering human life entangled lay
   Among the tightening coils of its own past ;
The Gardener came, the fetters fell away,
   The life unfolded to the sun at last.

HYMN FOR CHRISTMAS EVE.

MIGHTY world is hushed to-night
    In sweet expectancy;
O'er snowy field and wood the
    stainless light
Of the clear moon
Shines broad and free;
While peacefully the earth —
    A great white throne
Prepared for One who soon
Shall rise and claim it for His own —
    Awaits His birth.

The hearts of all mankind are turned
    Toward lowly Bethlehem;
For in the east the wondrous Star, that burned
    In days of old,
    Still beckons them.

Back o'er the centuries,
    Storm-swept and bare,
    It moves, until, behold!
It stands above the manger where
    The Young Child lies.

O Christmas chimes, right joyfully
    Ring out the tidings glad
To stars and frosty air and listening sky, —
    "Good-will to men!"
    Till all the sad,
The weary and oppressed,
    Their gifts shall bring
    To Him whose birth again
Sheds peace on earth, and, worshipping,
    Shall be at rest.

BLIND.

THROUGHOUT the weary day an Eastern sun
  Had poured his beams upon the whitened walls
Of Jericho, till e'en the drooping palms
Refused to comfort with their wonted shade
The passer-by. As in a furnace blast —
The glaring pavement spread beneath, o'erhead
A brazen, cloudless sky — all living things
Had gasped, with parching lips, and feebly prayed
For night.
      'T was eventide; the northern hills
Breathed forth a blessing on the multitude
That thronged incessant through the city gates.

Softly the mist crept forth, and o'er their
    heads
Her dewy wings unfolded. In the west
The molten brass of noontide turned to gold,
And shone like some fair missal's page, with
    hymns
And promises illumined.
                    One there was
Among the restless souls beneath its glow,
For whom the heavenly message was not
    writ;
For whom no sunset gleamed, nor morning
    dawned.
Oft had he listened to the merry shout
And laughter of the children at their sports,
But ne'er had looked upon their sparkling
    eyes.
Alone, he walked in darkness through a life
Of nights, with never hope of day. But
    hark!
Upon his ear there falls a gentle voice,
Whose tones of strange and heavenly sweet-
    ness thrill
His very heart. "'T is Jesus, 't is the Christ
Of Nazareth!" The woes of heavy years,

The quick-born hope, the old-time, dull despair,
The agony of help so near at hand,
Yet passing, blend in one wild, bitter cry:
"Jesus, thou Son of David, I am blind!
Have mercy on me!"—and the Saviour hears.
Blind Bartimeus by the road-side waits
In anguish mute and trembling, when, O joy!
The bringer of glad tidings is at hand:
"Be of good comfort, rise, he calleth thee!"

O weary, heavy-laden one, whose eyes
Have long been sightless to behold the truth, —
Perchance in darkness walking even now,
And longing with an aching heart for light, —
The Master's message echoes sweetly still:
"Be of good comfort, rise, He calleth thee."
And humbly kneeling at His feet, the words
Of healing, spoken in the olden time
To him who prayed for help, thou too shalt hear:
"Receive thy sight, thy faith hath made thee whole."

REFUGE.

OW bad I am, O Lord, Thou knowest,
  Deserving naught that Thou bestowest,
    But wandering each day
      Astray.

Thy gifts are perfect, never ceasing,
The debt against me still increasing,
    And yet I turn to flee
      From Thee!

Oft when my path is dark and narrow
There flutters down some tiny sparrow
    To tell me of that love
      Above.

In the Morning.

When daylight comes, I 'm e'er forgetting
The message sweet; my sins besetting
   Return, my soul to stain
    Again.

And so I cling to Thee, my Saviour,
Despairing by my own behavior
   To cleanse myself from sin
    Within.

My cares I yield — for me Thou carest;
I take my cross — its weight Thou sharest;
   Henceforth my will be Thine,
    Not mine.

GUIDO RENI'S "ECCE HOMO."

THORN-CROWNED head, the
    sins of all the world
  Have pierced thy brow;
O gentle face, the woes of all the world
    Thou bearest now!

O patient eyes, to heaven in meekness
  turned,
    Meekness divine,
Within your suffering depths what wondrous
  light
    Of love doth shine!

O faltering, parted lips, with anguish wrung,
    Your words still live
And plead for us, — "They know not what
  they do —
    Father, forgive!"

ON CHRISTMAS EVE.

HE day's loud footfalls die away,
And stealing forth from her retreat
Like a hooded nun, the twilight gray
Glides softly down the busy street.
With healing touch her gentle hand
Rests on the city's fevered brow;
Its throbbing pulse is quiet now,
And peace descends on the weary land.
Since morn the dull December sky
Has wept and moaned incessantly;
The tall, gaunt forms of shivering trees
Have groaned and rattled their bony arms,
Till, startled by the restless breeze,
The withered sprites of summer leaves
Have gathered to whisper their vague alarms,
Now whirling aloft to the dripping eaves,

On Christmas Eve.

Now wavering slow to earth again,
Borne down by the pitiless, hopeless rain.
Upon my hearth the ruddy light
Dances and plays at the fire-dogs' feet
Chasing the shadows out of sight;
Around the walls it follows them fast,
Hunts them into a corner at last,
Up the chimney, out into the night.
The blaze laughs loud with a music sweet,
My heart grows warm in its cheery glow,
And a thousand fancies come and go.
The perfumed breath of the birchen brand,
Rich with forest spices rare,
Bears heavenward many a hope and prayer
That only One can understand.
Oh that my life were sweet and pure
As the incense of this burning wood!
Oh that my faith were strong and sure
As the flame that ever strives toward God!
I hear the sound of the sleet and rain
Brushing against my window-pane;
The voice of the wind is sad and low,
The shadows return, and to and fro
They flit and hover uneasily,
Until at last they rest on me.

Heap high the sturdy fire-dogs' backs
With boughs of hemlock, birch, and pine.
The crisp bark curls, and smokes, and cracks;
It comes at last, the spark divine,
And bursting forth in broad, free laughter,
The glorious blaze comes hurrying after,
Springs up the chimney with a roar,
Chasing the shadows away once more,
Shining far out upon the floor,
And sweeping away on its gladsome tide
The fears and doubts, o'er which I sighed,
To the depths of the sea, to the depths of
    the sea, —
The cares and sins that have haunted me!

I thank thee for thy help, sweet hour,
For thou hast helped me true and well;
I thank thee for the gentle spell
Beneath which thou dost wield thy power,
And when the twilight seeks at morn
Her convent walls within the west,
My soul shall know its truest rest,
And bless the day when Christ was born.

BY NIGHT.

    'ER Judah's dark hill-tops the star-
        light is shining;
    In silence the silvery light
Falls soft on the white, sleeping lambs and
    their shepherds,
        By night.

Sleep on, trustful flocks, while shepherds are
    watching;
    Fear not, for soon shall be born
The dear Lamb of God, in a Bethlehem
    manger,
        This morn.

Keep watch, faithful shepherds, through gath-
    ering shadows,
    Though the hillside be lonely and drear;
For lo, in the darkness the Shepherd of shep-
    herds
        Is near!

Sing on, ye bright angels, repeat the glad
    tidings, —
  Joy, peace, and good-will on the earth;
Proclaim to the weary, the sad, and the suffer-
    ing,
        His birth.

Shine, radiant Star in the East, till thy glory
    O'er Wise Men and manger is poured,
For Mary's dear babe is the blessed Christ
    Jesus,
        Our Lord.

"STAR OF BETHLEHEM."

GENTLE-FACED child-flower —
   One of the least —
Dost thou remember
   The Star in the East,
Bethlehem's hill-tops
   Flushing with morn,
When in a manger
   The dear Christ was born?

Lambs on the hillside
   Peacefully slept;
Shepherds, abiding near,
   Faithful watch kept.
Bright in the heavens
   Shone a new star,
Guiding o'er deserts
   Wise Men from afar.

In the Morning.

White Flower of Bethlehem,
    Lo, it is morn!
Shine on the manger
    Where Jesus was born.
We, too, shall find Him,
    Though humblest and least,
Led by thy radiance,
    Bright Star in the East.

"BLESSED."

"BLESSED are they that mourn."
    The gentle tones,
    A moment faltering, then strong
      and sweet,
Ring out upon the morning air.   The throng
Wait silently, lest by a whispered sigh
Or quick-drawn breath a word should fall unheard
From Him, the wonderful, the Prince of Peace.
" Blessed " — the widow, shuddering, draws more close
Her sombre draperies, and bows her head
In agony of dumb and hopeless grief.

— " Are they that mourn ! " A dry, half-stifled sob
Bursts from a gray-haired man ; 't was yesterday

They buried all most dear to him on earth,
And sun and stars were blotted out. Hot tears
Fall thickly on his knotted, sunburnt hands,
And still he listens to that strange, sweet voice.

"Blessed are they that mourn." What aching hearts
Among the eager, silent multitude
Cry out in bitter anguish that His words
Are vain and mocking !
      Lo, the Saviour turns
With infinite compassion in His eye,
And stretching forth His hands as though to give
The blessing He has promised, speaks again :
"They shall be comforted !"

       The morning sun
Breaks forth in triumph from the heavy clouds
That hid His face. The waves of Galilee,
Gleaming far distant in the misty east,
Cast off the shroud of night. The air is full
Of waking glory. But of all who feel

The gladness and the freshness of the morn,
Those only who have passed through deep-
    est gloom
Receive the fulness of that new, sweet peace
His words have given, — and they are com-
    forted!

A CHRISTMAS PASTORAL.

THE shepherds were keeping their watch by night,
  In the field with their flock abiding;
And soft on the fleece of the lambs fell the light
    Of a new-risen star,
    From deserts afar
  The wise ones to Bethlehem guiding.

What startles the watchers? A rustle of wings,
  And a radiant figure above them.
The lambs are afraid, and the white, woolly things,
    With tremulous bleat,
    Nestle close to the feet
  Of the faithful shepherds who love them.

"Fear not!" comes the message, exultant
and strong,
"Good tidings of joy I am bringing!"
And lo! with the song of a heavenly throng,
"Peace on earth! For this morn
A Saviour is born!"
The hillsides of Judah are ringing.

The bright ones are gone; over thicket and
stone
The starlight of Christmas is falling;
But the lambs, without even an angel, alone
In the great silent night,
With sudden affright,
For their lost shepherds vainly are calling.

They knew not a tenderer Shepherd was near,
His flocks to deliver from danger,
And comfort all desolate lambs in their fear, —
For peacefully lay,
On that first Christmas day,
Lord Christ, in a Bethlehem manger.

THE FOURTH WATCH.

MIDNIGHT upon Gennesaret; the restless waves,
　　Like jewels on the troubled bosom of the sea,
Flash forth in rays of silvery light, or hide within
Her dark and flowing tresses. Soft, as in a dream,
The night-winds sigh and whisper o'er the little ship,
While from the far-off, shadowy hills of Galilee
Their cool breath gently fans the weary twelve, as rests
A loving hand upon a fevered, aching brow.
Deserted lies the quiet, moon-lit shore, but all

The Fourth Watch.

The air is heavy with the perfume of the grass,
Crushed into fragrance by the waiting multitude
Whom Jesus fed. The Giver of the bread of life
Has gone apart upon the mountain-side to pray,
Alone.
  The night is dark, the Master is not come;
The sea arises, and on every side the waves
Gigantic, black, and topped with lurid crests of foam,
Leap madly through the gloom. Labors the little ship,
Hurled to and fro and beaten back upon her course.
With slow and stubborn stroke the rowers wearily
Are straining at the heavy oars. But hark! above
The sullen roar of wind and sea, a well-loved voice,

Vibrant and sweet with chords of heavenly
  music, speaks,
And they were sore afraid; but He saith
  unto them,
" Be of good cheer, 't is I, be not afraid."
  And lo,
The tempest ceased! and when they had
  received their Lord,
The ship had come unto the haven they
  desired.

"WITH YOU ALWAY."

WHY seek ye for Jehovah
   Mid Sinai's awful smoke?
   The burning bush now shelters
A sparrow's humble folk;
The curve of God's sweet heaven
Is the curve of the leaf of oak;
The Voice that stilled the tempest
To little children spoke,—
The bread of life eternal
Is the bread He blessed and broke.

DECEMBER 31.

ANOTHER year!
    What is the story by the twelve-
        month told?
What treasure doth its memory enfold, —
    Base coin, or gold?
Sternly hath it hard lessons taught,
Hath it new cares, new joys, new burdens
        brought?
    Few smiles, and many a tear?

    Another year!
What good and perfect gifts have gently
        come —
Knowing not whence, we have been blind
        and dumb!
    We ate the crumb
Without the sparrow's faith, but still,
Father of Lights, Thou shinest on, and will,
    Thy frightened birds to cheer.

December 31.

Another year!
The sunlight pours its blessings as of old,
Into the lap of each dear day, — its gold,
　　Its wealth untold.
As lessons new and sweet we gain,
Still hoping to the highest to attain,
　　We trust, and never fear.

Another year!
But to the brave and true, lo, time is not!
A thousand years are as a day, forgot
　　The hardest lot,
To those who walk beside their God,
Loving the path His patient feet have trod,
　　Knowing that He is near.

IN MY ARM-CHAIR.

FLICKERS the ruddy firelight on the
    wall;
Now here, now there, the shadows
    restlessly
Dance in and out among the gleaming bars
That prison many a glimpse of sea and sky
Upon the pictured canvas. Brightly falls
The cheerful light upon familiar forms
Of volumes clothed in sober garb and gay,
Whose very names, in golden characters,
Invite to solace sweet, and peace of mind.
Footfalls incessant in the rainy street
Mingle their dreary cadence with the roll
And rhythmic echo of the iron wheel,
Half muffled by the storm's dull monotone.
Within, the gentle presence of the flame,
With its soft rustle ever and anon,

Serves but to take away the very pain
Of silence absolute.
     It is the hour
For contemplation meet. The air is thronged
With thoughts innumerable, fancies light,
That flit about on airy wing, or play
Among the fireborn shadows on the wall;
Till, touched by the Promethean glow, they
  take
A seeming form substantial, animate.
From out their thin octavo cells pour forth
The shapes ethereal of poet, sage,
Philosopher, and man of God, whose words
Make wisdom beautiful, and beauty wise.
Silent they rise before me, one by one,
E'en as the fabled genius, close involved
Within the tiny casket, gained at last
His proper self, and towered high above
His liberator. But of other mien
Are these strange forms around my hearth
  to-night.
With aspect grave, yet kind, they gaze on me
As old companions might on one they loved,
Who loved them in return. I know each one,

And recognize the habit of his life.
Old Gilbert White — whose flowing locks,
    and dress
Of quaint antiquity, precise and neat,
Recall his quiet walks in Selborne wood —
Has paused with curious, meditative eye,
Before an owl upon my mantle shelf,
And rapidly, in shadowy script, records
The sapient bird's presentment.
                              Near at hand,
A man of kindly countenance and mild,
Impressed with lines of pure and noble
    thought,
Bends low in prayer; ere long resumes his
    pen,
And adds one more sweet hymn to those
    that bear
George Herbert's name. Anon appears a face
More gentle than the rest, it seems, with eyes
Of deep and tender yearning. Silently
The figure turns aside, and by the hearth
Remains aloof, with dreamy gaze intent
Upon the glowing coals. What fantasies
Are imaged there, reflected from his mind,

And striving for the elixir of his touch
And wondrous pen, that give eternal life
To such as they! Lo, built of candent fire
The Old Manse drops its Mosses at his feet;
Italia's strange physician whispers now
Of potent herb and flower. The Puritan,
His wonted sternness softened, deigns to tell
Of old-time guilt— the Scarlet Letter's brand—
Till, glancing up, he shudders at the approach
Of stricken Hester, with her demon child.

So wanes the night. In quick succession move
Shades of the mighty dead before my eyes.
Again is played the Comedy Divine,
And gloomily the awful form of him
Whose mind such Titan offspring bore, attends
The movement of each scene. The cowl and robe,
Close at his side, betray that zealous monk
Whose life was Imitation of the Christ.
Amid the still increasing throng, behold
Sage Izaak Walton, creel and rod in hand;
But while I gaze upon his visage mild,

Expectant half to hear his counsel how
The wily carp to ensnare, the fiery bridge
O'er which my fancy boldly trod, and found
Her way to realms unreal, topples down
With mimic crash, and lies a ruined mass
Upon the hearth. Yet by its waning glow
I see the hurried parting of my guests,
Retreating each within his narrow cell;
As when beneath a monastery roof
The low, sweet chant of vespers dies away, —
The last faint echoes lingering still within
The moonlit cloisters, — silently the forms
Of holy men glide to and fro among
The shadows, till the hush of night descends
With brooding wings, and gathers all to rest.

THE END.

www.ingramcontent.com/pod-product-compliance
Lightning Source LLC
Chambersburg PA
CBHW030309170426
43202CB00009B/931